C.1

What is wind?

Robin Johnson

🌳 Crabtree Publishing Company
www.crabtreebooks.com

Author
Robin Johnson

Publishing plan research and development
Sean Charlebois, Reagan Miller
Crabtree Publishing Company

Editors
Reagan Miller, Crystal Sikkens

Proofreader
Kathy Middleton

Photo research
Crystal Sikkens

Design
Ken Wright

Production coordinator
and prepress technician
Ken Wright

Print coordinator
Katherine Berti

Photographs
Shutterstock: front cover, pages 4, 5, 13, 14, 16,
    18 (left and top right), 21
Thinkstock: back cover, pages 1, 3, 6, 7, 8, 9, 10, 11,
    12, 15, 17, 18 (except left and top right), 19, 20, 22

Library and Archives Canada Cataloguing in Publication

Johnson, Robin (Robin R.)
    What is wind? / Robin Johnson.

(Weather close-up)
Includes index.
Issued also in electronic formats.
ISBN 978-0-7787-0757-8 (bound).--ISBN 978-0-7787-0764-6 (pbk.)

    1. Winds--Juvenile literature.
I. Title. II. Series: Weather close-up

QC931.4.J64 2012   j551.51'8   C2012-903949-7

Library of Congress Cataloging-in-Publication Data

CIP available at Library of Congress

Crabtree Publishing Company

www.crabtreebooks.com   1-800-387-7650

Printed in Hong Kong/092012/BK20120629

Published in Canada
Crabtree Publishing
616 Welland Ave.
St. Catharines, Ontario
L2M 5V6

Published in the United States
Crabtree Publishing
PMB 59051
350 Fifth Avenue, 59th Floor
New York, New York 10118

Published in the United Kingdom
Crabtree Publishing
Maritime House
Basin Road North, Hove
BN41 1WR

Published in Australia
Crabtree Publishing
3 Charles Street
Coburg North
VIC 3058

Contents

What is wind?

Wind is moving air. We cannot see the wind, but we can see the wind move things. It blows leaves and bends the branches of trees. It lifts kites high into the air and turns umbrellas inside out. We can feel the wind on our skin and in our hair. Sometimes we can even hear the wind howl!

What do you think?

What clues in this picture show it is a windy day?

4

Windy weather

The wind is part of **weather**. Weather is what the air and sky are like each day. Weather is always changing. Some days the weather is cool and **breezy**. Other days the weather is warm and the wind is calm.

Wind can keep you cool on a hot, sunny day and make you feel colder on a cold, snowy day.

What makes the wind blow?

Wind is made by differences in air **temperature**. The Sun heats the ground. The ground warms the air above it. As the air gets warmer, it becomes lighter. The warm, light air rises high in the sky. As the warm air rises, cooler air moves in under it to take its place. This moving air is the wind.

Have you ever seen a bird rise up in the air without flapping its wings? The bird is using the warm, rising air to lift it high in the sky.

Air pressure

Air is all around you. Air has weight and takes up space. **Air pressure** is the weight of the air that presses down on Earth. Cool air has high pressure. Warm air has low pressure. Air moves from an area of high pressure to an area of low pressure. If the difference between the high and low pressure areas is small, the wind is a gentle breeze. If the difference is great, the wind is stronger.

What do you think?

Is the difference in air pressure small or great in this picture?

High to low

A **meteorologist** is a scientist who studies and measures weather. Meteorologists study air pressure to learn where the wind will blow and how strong it will be. They use a tool called a **barometer** to measure air pressure. High air pressure means cool and dry weather. Low air pressure means warm and wet weather.

low pressure

high pressure

Cool tools

Meteorologists use many tools to measure the wind. They use **anemometers** to measure wind speed. Wind makes the cups on an anemometer spin. The cups spin slowly when the wind moves slowly. The cups spin quickly when the wind moves quickly. A meteorologist counts the number of times an anemometer spins to measure the speed of the wind.

Wind speed is measured in miles per hour or kilometers per hour.

Vanes and socks

Meteorologists use **wind vanes** and **wind socks** to measure wind direction. Sometimes a change in wind direction is a sign that the weather is changing. A wind sock has a large and a small opening at either end. The wind blows in through the large opening and out through the small opening. The wind turns the sock in the direction the wind is blowing.

A wind vane has an arrow that points in the direction from which the wind is blowing.

Turn to page 18 to learn how to make your own wind sock.

11

Windstorms

Learning about the wind helps meteorologists **predict** what the weather will be. To predict is to tell what will happen before it takes place. The wind can tell whether rain clouds are moving into an area or if there are clear skies ahead. It also helps meteorologists predict if there are big windstorms on the way. Then meteorologists can warn people about the storms so they can stay safe.

This family is putting boards on their windows to protect them from a windstorm coming their way.

Tornados are very powerful winds that can destroy homes and cars.

Wild winds

Hurricanes are large storms with very strong winds. They bring heavy rain and last for days. They can destroy trees, cars, and buildings. **Tornados** are storms with very strong, swirling clouds of wind. They last for only a few minutes, but can do a lot of damage.

Wind power

Some windmills are still used today.

Wind can also be very helpful. People have been using wind power for many years. Long ago, people began using **windmills** to grind grain into flour. Today, people use wind to make **energy**. Energy is the power to make things work. We use energy to heat and light our homes.

14

How does the wind make energy?

People use large machines called **wind turbines** to make energy. The blades of a wind turbine turn when the wind blows. The blades connect to a motor inside the wind turbine. When the blades turn, the motor turns. The motor makes energy for people to use.

*These wind turbines are making energy on a **wind farm**.*

Gone with the wind

What do you think?

The wind is pushing this sailboat across the water. What else does the wind move?

The wind is always moving things from place to place. It can carry a balloon high into the sky or make leaves dance in the air. The wind can blow a piece of paper out of your hand and make you run to try and catch it.

Changing the world

The wind spreads seeds so plants can grow in new places. At the same time, the wind blows away soil. Less soil makes it hard for farmers to grow plants. The wind also carries away tiny pieces of rock from the land. Over time, the wind changes the shape of Earth.

The wind wears away rock and creates different shapes called hoodoos.

Be a wind watcher!

Follow these steps to make a wind sock. Your wind sock will show you the direction the wind blows each day!

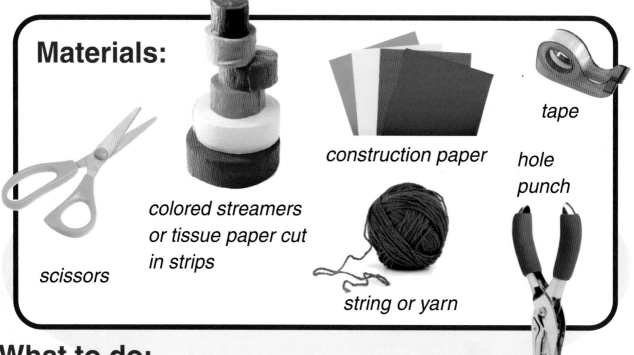

Materials:

scissors

colored streamers or tissue paper cut in strips

construction paper

string or yarn

tape

hole punch

What to do:

1. Tape the long edges of a sheet of construction paper together, creating a tube with holes at both ends.

2. Cut the tissue paper or streamers into a few long strips.

3. Tape the tissue paper strips onto one end of the construction-paper tube.

4. Punch two holes in the other end of the tube. The holes should be across from each other.

5. Cut off a long piece of string. Thread one end through a hole and tie a knot. Do the same with the other end.

6. Use the string to hang your wind sock from a tree branch, clothesline, or other safe place outside.

Now you are ready to be a wind watcher!

Look and learn

Look at your wind sock at the same time each day. Use a **compass** to find out in which direction the wind is blowing the sock. A compass is a tool that shows directions, such as east and west. Does your wind sock always blow in the same direction? Does the wind change direction during the day? Can you tell how strong the wind is blowing by watching your wind sock? How?

Show and tell

Write down what you see in a **weather journal**. A weather journal is a notebook you use to write about the wind and other weather each day. You can draw pictures of the weather in your journal, too! Later, you can make a chart to show your friends all the cool things you learned about the wind. It will really blow them away!

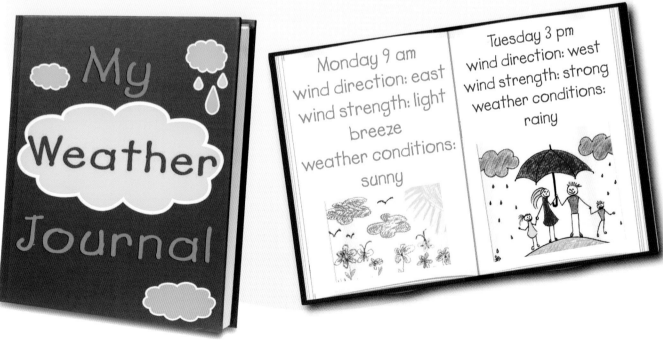

Monday 9 am
wind direction: east
wind strength: light breeze
weather conditions: sunny

Tuesday 3 pm
wind direction: west
wind strength: strong
weather conditions: rainy

Charting wind

Devon watched the wind and weather at his house for a whole week. He recorded the **data**, or information, in his weather journal. He then used the data to make a chart to show his friends. Look at the data on Devon's wind chart and answer these questions:

1. What direction did the wind most often blow from?

2. Which days were good days for Devon to fly a kite?

3. Do you see a connection between the wind direction and the weather?

Day	Time					
	9:00 am			3:00 pm		
	Wind Direction	Wind Strength	Weather Condition	Wind Direction	Wind Strength	Weather Condition
Mon.	south	light breeze	sunny	south	strong breeze	sun and clouds
Tue.	south	strong breeze	sunny	south	light wind	cloudy
Wed.	south	strong breeze	cloudy	west	light wind	light rain
Thu.	west	strong wind	cloudy	north	strong wind	thunder-storm
Fri.	south	light breeze	sun and clouds	south	light breeze	sunny
Sat.	south	strong breeze	sun and clouds	east	light wind	cloudy
Sun.	east	light wind	light rain	south	calm	sunny

Find out more

Books

Changing Weather: Storms by Kelley MacAulay and Bobbie Kalman. Crabtree Publishing Company, 2006.

Now we know about the weather by Mike Goldsmith. Crabtree Publishing Company, 2009.

What is climate? (Big Science Ideas) by Bobbie Kalman. Crabtree Publishing Company, 2012.

Wind and Storms by Robyn Hardyman. PowerKids Press, 2010.

Wind Power (Energy for Today) by Tea Benduhn. Gareth Stevens Publishing, 2008.

Websites

Energy Kids: Renewable Wind

www.eia.gov/kids/energy.cfm?page=wind_home-basics

Weather Wiz Kids

www.weatherwizkids.com/weather-wind.htm

Glossary

Note: Some boldfaced words are defined where they appear in the book.

air pressure (air PRESH-er) *noun* The force of air pushing on things

anemometer (an-uh-MOM-i-ter) *noun* A tool that shows the speed and pressure of wind

barometer (buh-ROM-i-ter) *noun* A tool that shows air pressure

breezy (BREE-zee) *adjective* Windy

temperature (TEHM-per-a-chur) *noun* How cold or warm the air is

wind farm (WIND-fahrm) *noun* An area of land with a group of wind turbines used to make electricity

windmill (WIND-mil) *noun* A building with large sails that uses wind power to run a machine

wind sock (WIND-sok) *noun* A tool that shows which way and how hard the wind blows

wind turbine (WIND TUR-bahyn) *noun* A machine that uses wind power to make energy

wind vane (WIND-veyn) *noun* A tool that shows which way the wind blows

A noun is a person, place, or thing. An adjective is a word that tells you what something is like.

Index